A BIT OF CRACK FROM BELFAST

DOREEN McBRIDE

CONTENTS

Give Us a Bit of Yer Crack	1
Essential Vocabulary	6
Belfast Crack	8
Miscellaneous Snatches Overheard in Many Places	17
Troubled Times	20
Terrible Tales	27
The Industrial Scene	36
The Only Place For Me	47

Reform Club, Royal Avenue

GIVE US A BIT OF YER CRACK

I was born in Belfast and I love it. To me it is a beautiful city, full of friendly people and full of crack. It is a city that is said to have inspired Jonathan Swift to write 'Gulliver's Travels' as he looked at the outline of the Antrim Hills from a distance and thought they looked like the profile of a sleeping giant. It is a city with a fine tradition of wall sculpture and sign writing which has not been entirely obliterated by modern notions of signs and neon lights. It is a city whose inhabitants regard it with pride and a city of courage which may be bloodied but will not be bowed, whose people in the face of adversity pick themselves up, dust themselves down and crack a joke.

Belfast people speak a dialect of the language known locally as 'Norn Iron'. 'Norn Iron' itself is a version of the best English ever spoken, as explained in my locally best selling book *'Speakin Norn Iron As She Shud be Spoke'*. Visitors may find it difficult to understand, but it is worth persevering and listening carefully so that an appreciation of the richness of the language can be developed.

Traditional sign writing, Belfast

Wall sculpture on a building in Belfast

It is a city of serious and quirky "Poets" such as Crawford Howard who wrote 'St. Patrick and the Snakes'.

ST. PATRICK AND THE SNAKES

You've heard of the snakes in Australia,
You've heard of the snakes in Japan,
You've heard of the rattler — that old Texas battler —
Whose bite can mean death to a man.
They've even got snakes in old England —
Nasty adders all yellow and black —
But in Erin's green Isle we can say with a smile
They're away — and they're not coming back!

Now years ago things was quite different —
There was serpents all over the place.
If ye climbed up a ladder ye might meet an adder,
Or a cobra might lep at your face,
If ye went for a walk up the Shankill,
Or a dander along Sandy Row,
A flamin' great python would likely come withrin'
An' take a lump outa yer toe!

New there once was a guy called St. Patrick,
A preacher of fame and renown —
An' he hoisted his sails and came over from Wales
To convert all the heathens in Down,
An' he hirpled about through the country
With a stick an' a big pointy hat,
An' he kept a few sheep that he sold on the cheap,
But sure there's no money in that!

He was preachin' a sermon in Comber
An gettin' quite carried away
An' he mentioned that Rome had once been his home
(But that was the wrong thing to say!)
For he felt a sharp pain in his cheek–bone
An' he stuck up a hand 'till his bake
An' the thing that had lit on his gub (an' had bit)
Was a wee Presbyterian snake!

Now the snake slithered down from the pulpit
(Expectin' St. Patrick to die),
But yer man was no dozer — he lifted his crozier
An' he belted the snake in the eye,
And he says till the snake, 'Listen legless!
You'd just better take yerself aff!
If you think that that trick will work with St. Patrick
You must be far worser nor daft!

So the snake slithered home in a temper
An' it gathered its friends all aroun'
An' it says, 'Listen, mates! We'll get on wer skates,
I reckon it's time to leave town!
It's no fun when you bite a big fella
An' sit back and expect him to die
An' he's so flamin' quick with thon big, crooked stick
That he hits ye a dig in the eye!

So a strange sight confronted St. Patrick
When he work up the very next day.
The snakes with long faces were all packin' their cases
An' headin' for Donegall Quay.
Some got on cheap flights to Majorca
And some booked apartments in Spain.
They were all headin' out and there wasn't a doubt
That they weren't going to come back again.

So the reason the snakes left old Ireland,
(An' this is no word of a lie),
They all went to places to bite people's face
And be reasonably sure that they'd die.
An' the oul' snakes still caution their grandsons,
'For God's sake beware of St. Pat!
An' take yerselves aff if you see his big staff,
An' his cloak, an' his big pointy hat!'

Crawford Howard

In Belfast people often strike up conversations with strangers and tell them wonderful things such as:

'The wathers shackin'! It's been comin' down stair rods for weeks!'

'Do ye see my oul man? He hasn't an ounce.'

'It's lovely between the rain.'

Belfast streets provide plenty of crack!
The word 'crack' was brought in from the British mainland in the eighteenth century and became part of the local language. It has disappeared from mainland Britain and its meaning is difficult to explain to strangers although everyone in Ireland knows precisely what it means. It refers to talk, light hearted chat, banter, usually, but not always, with an emphasis on fun. Americans will be relieved to know it has nothing to do with drugs! A couple of visiting Americans thought Belfast (and Dublin) were terrible cities because, as they explained, 'Places like pubs are covered in signs saying things like "Come in for the Crack", "The Best Crack in Town", "We Are Famous For Our Crack" and policemen simply walk past and do nothing about it!" To put it in common parlance, locals nearly laughed their legs off!

There is a move to spell 'crack' as 'craic to avoid confusion. 'Crack' was the original version so 'crack it remains as far as this book is concerned.

Crack takes many forms such as chat, storytelling, reciting a monologue, and so on.

The Irish are a nation of storytellers and that is particularly true of those living in Belfast. It is impossible for a day to pass among people in Belfast without hearing at least one story. Enjoy the crack by becoming an eavesdropper, or better still, join in! Strangers are welcome and anyone prepared to talk is appreciated. Buses, black taxis, queues, pubs and restaurants are all fertile places for lively talk. Enjoy the rich flow of descriptive language, the play on words, the humour and the sense of fun expressed. The later the hour the better the crack.

This book is the result of years spent as a conscientious eavesdropper. I suggest you read the dialect sections aloud, memorise a couple of stories choosing a favourite, re-read it a couple of times, visualise it like a video, then tell it to somebody. Never attempt to learn a story off by heart, just remember the beginning, the middle and the end. The words will probably change slightly each time it is told and that does not matter. People in Belfast, and indeed in the rest of Ireland, appreciate stories and will probably tell one in return. Before you know where you are you will be having quare crack. Try sharing the monologues with friends, either by reading them aloud, or better still, learning them off by heart and reciting them. Enjoy the crack!

Do ye see my oul man?
He hasn't an ounce

ESSENTIAL VOCABULARY

It is always pleasant to know a few words of the native tongue when visiting a foreign place because, with the exception of the French who have fussy notions regarding pronunciation, natives appreciate an attempt to speak their language. Belfast people love their own special dialect of Norn Iron, the language commonly spoken in the North of Ireland. Strangers uttering, or responding to, the following words and phrases will delight Belfast folk who are patient and helpful, correcting pronunciation and extending vocabulary. It is a rare visitor who leaves Belfast without, at the very least, being able to utter that locally well known phrase 'Dead on!'

'Bout ye	Derived from 'How's about ye?' or 'Wot about ye?'. Means 'How are you?'
Cowl	Cold
Dead on	I am fine, better than 100%.
Geg	Joke
Gub	Mouth
Hermit	This word is of comparatively recent origin. It arose from black taxi drivers' habit of saying 'Here, Miss' or 'Here, Mister' when giving change to customers. 'Hermit' is an economical word as it is equally suitable for use with male or female clients.
Sam	So I am.
Sodoeye	So do I. This is another word derived from a common habit in Norn Iron, namely speaking so quickly that words run into each other forming a portmanteau word.

Stickin' out	That's excellent
Thon wos quare crack	That was great fun.
Thon thonder	Over there.
Yer flyin' tonight	You have had too much to drink.
Yous gettin?'	Are you being served.
Wud yew like a wee cup av tea in yur han?	Would you like a cup of tea? (This will be served as you sit in a comfortable chair, but not at a formally set table. The polite response is to say, without conviction, 'No, thank you very much. It's too much trouble.' Then allow yourself to be persuaded to take tea. Belfast people, and indeed those from the rest of Ireland, are surprised and disappointed when visiting other cultures when they refuse refreshment and then receive none!

It's a geg

BELFAST CRACK

An old friend, called Martha, epitomised what I love best about Belfast people. She was a wee, warm woman who used to sit by her fire and giggle. The giggle would explode into a hearty roar which reduced the rest of the family to hysterics. She died in 1982 in the house in which she had been born and my daughter said, through her tears, 'I'll always remember Martha sitting by the fire laughing.' That is how I remember her too and it is how I think of countless other Belfast women

Martha lived in a 'two-up-two down' house in Bloomfield Street, off East Bread Street in East Belfast. The house is still there although the area has since been redeveloped. In her later years she developed high blood pressure and became afraid to go into the city centre. "My head becomes dizzy," she explained, "and I'm scared of falling." We missed her tales of derring-do about visits into Belfast city centre, but she managed to keep us in crack about things which happened around the street. Here are some of her stories. It has been said that 'you are the story that you tell'. The type of story told by Martha is similar to that told by countless other Belfast people, gentle, full of humour and kindliness.

THE DAY THE MORONS CAME

There was a period when the neighbourhood was invaded by what Martha referred to as 'them morons'. She meant Mormons - like all Belfast people she loved to play on words. The 'morons', dressed in good suits, went from door to door looking for converts. They were wasting their time. The majority of the people in the street were conventional, good living Christians, who attended church twice on Sundays and then went to meetings in the local missionary hall a couple of times a week. Attempting to import any type of Christianity to Bloomfield Street was like bringing coals to Newcastle.

Martha watched the 'morons' as they travelled from door to door along the street. Eventually they rapped loudly on next door neighbour Mrs. Spratt's door. Mrs. Spratt, when roused, had a bit of a temper and she had been complaining about previous attempts to evangelise her. 'Them ones have a right cheek! I'm not going to be evangelised!' she had proclaimed. 'What do they think I am? A heathen? At my age?' She flung the door open with such vigour that it bounced against the thin wall of Martha's house causing it to shake. 'The whole house shook,' she recalled, her eyes twinkling with amusement. 'The window shook, the walls shook, even the clock on the mantelpiece shook. I thought it was going to fall on the floor!'

'What do you want?' screamed Mrs. Spratt, so loudly the whole street could hear her.

'We've come to tell you about Jesus,' quavered one of the 'morons'.

'Get to hell out of it!' screeched Mrs. Spratt. 'Ah'm a Christian!'

THE DAY MARTHA FELL, UNDER THE BED

High blood pressure made Martha unsteady whenever she stood up, especially first thing in the morning when she got out of bed. She never complained, but would say with a smile, 'My head feels funny. I should feel my back instead!'

One morning, after a good night's sleep, Martha climbed out of the large double bed in the front bedroom. She felt dizzy and sat on the bed in her nightdress. She wiggled her toes as the doctor had suggested. The dizziness persisted. The weather was chilly and the house did not have central heating. Martha felt cold. 'I'd better get dressed,' she thought. She stood up, took off her nightdress and began to struggle into her ample corset. She broke out in a sweat, began to feel sick, fainted and fell under the bed.

'I thought I was dying,' she explained to us the next time we visited. 'I was very disappointed. I always thought your whole life flashed in front of your eyes when you're dying. I've even heard of people who saw angels, heard beautiful singing and had a glimpse of heaven. Well, do you know what I saw? I saw the ambulance coming to the door and the ambulance men climbing up the stairs and finding me and the state I was in. Do you know what they saw? They saw "up America", that's what they saw! I'm too old at my age to let anyone see "up America"!

'I didn't know where I was when I came round. I thought I was in hell. It was all black when I opened my eyes. I remember thinking "It's freezing here." I thought there were fires in hell. You live and learn! Then I started to laugh because I thought I was dead and "You die and learn" does not have the same ring. Then I realised I was lying with my head under the bed and the curtains were still closed. I was greatly relieved, I'm telling you. The ambulance men hadn't had the chance to see "up America"'.

SEE ME? SEE MY MAN? SEE CHEESE? CAN'T STAND IT!

One night Martha came back from her wee meeting in the mission hall. She was in stitches with laughter. 'It was a special night with a guest speaker, visitors and eats!' she explained. 'We had a lovely guest tea with sandwiches, currant loaf, cake and fresh cream buns. It was gorgeous! One of the visitors was a big fat woman. She went up to the table and looked at all the cheese sandwiches. She put her hands on her hips and said, "See me? See my man? See cheese? Can't stand it!" Poetry, I call that. Sheer poetry!'

Listening to people talk in Belfast is a pleasure. There is a rich vein of humour which pops up in unexpected places.

HOW LONG WILL THE NEXT BUS BE?

Martha once described how she had been in the city centre shopping. She went to the bus stop in Chichester Street and joined the queue for the Bloomfield bus. There was one woman in front of her. The pair, as often happens, struck up a conversation. The woman remembered an errand she had forgotten to do. She said it would not take her long, just a few minutes. At that moment the bus arrived. It was a double decker and this was in the days when each bus had a driver and a conductor.

The bus drew up at the stop, the conductor hung out the back and turned the handle to change the stated destination of the bus. The woman went up to him and inquired, 'How long will the next bus be?' (She meant, what length of time will elapse before the next bus is expected?)

The conductor, without even looking up, replied, 'It will be the just same length as this one!'

'And,' asked the woman, 'will it have a cheeky wee monkey turning its handle and all?'

The Old Belfast Waterworks, Belfast City Centre

AND THE CISTERN FELL ON HER HEAD

My sister come home on a bus one day and eavesdropped on what she described as 'two oul dolls' who were talking in solemn tones about a neighbour, called 'Aggie', who had suddenly become very frightened of life. She knew something awful was going to happen to her. She had had a premonition, so she stayed in the house to keep safe, never went out, stopped visiting her friends and generally led a dull, uninteresting life.

At this time, the late 50's many of the smaller houses in Belfast did not have proper bathrooms. People washed at the kitchen sink and had an occasional bath in front of the fire in a large zinc container which was stored in the small yard behind the house, carried in when required, placed in front of the fire and filled with water. This type of dwelling had an old fashioned toilet, with a high level cistern, housed at the end of the yard.

Poor Aggie went to the toilet. The pulled the chain, the cistern broke and fell on her head. She was knocked unconscious and suffered a fractured skull. According to the oul dolls, Aggie would have died from hypothermia, lying unconscious in the frost covered yard, if a neighbour had not heard the commotion and investigated.

Aggie was taken to hospital where she lay and bemoaned her fate. She said she just KNEW something awful was going to happen to her, so had taken precautions and not run risks. She told the 'oul dolls', 'The next time I have a premonition, I'm going out every day. I'll even go into the pub because I might as well!'

The communities of people living in little houses were very caring and supportive. Families lived in the same neighbourhood for generations, their neighbours were friends, a helping hand was always there in times of trouble, children were taught to be sociable and polite but without fear of adults. These places were destroyed by the development of high rise flats during the 50's and 60's. (The policy has now been reversed and it is to be hoped that other new community spirits will develop over the course of time.)

Seamus Lavery lived in such a community before he was married. Years later he met his mother walking up the road near their old home. She was in tears. Seamus asked her why she was crying and she explained that she had come out of her new high rise and gone to see her old house. She was just in time to watch it being knocked down. Seamus was so moved he went home and penned the following verses telling the story of his mother's 'wee house' from her view point. It paints a telling picture of life in the small houses of Belfast.

Inner City Belfast

MY WEE HOUSE

It was only a wee house, as wee houses go,
Two rooms upstairs and two down below,
With the door always open and no thought of danger,
But a warm friendly welcome for friend and for stranger.

Though it was only oil cloth that covered the floor,
It was always kept clean, aye, clean to be sure,
With a big wooden table I'd scrubbed almost white,
And a black-leaded grate, with fire burning bright.

It was not always tidy and not always neat
When the children played games on the floor at m'feet,
But least they were happy, as happy could be,
And that was the only thing that mattered to me.

It had no central heating, yet always was warm.
It kept us all safe through manys a storm,
And on cold winter nights round the fire we would sit.
While the children told stories I'd listen and knit.

On Saturday nights, with the wee ones all in,
I'd bring in the big bath, made out of tin.
When I had them all washed and safely in bed,
I would sit on the sofa and shower my poor head.

I didn't have much and what I had was soon gone,
But sure if I ran short there was always the pawn,
When the shoes and the clothes that we wore every Sunday,
Were cleaned and wrapped up for me 'Uncle's' on Monday.

Aye, them was the days that they say was hard,
When to go to the toilet, y'went to the yard,
And y'sat w' yer feet lifted off the floor,
When the rain or the snow blew under the door.

Ah, but many's the day when the sun would shine
We would go on a tram to the end of the line,
Where I'd sit on my shawl and think it was grand,
As m'children played games on the Greencastle sand.

And on warm winter evenings I would get m'wee stool,
And I'd sit at the door with m'needles and wool.
Sometimes I would knit and other times darn
While me and wee Cassie would have a quare yarn.

Then things started changing, for better or worse,
And some o'them changes t'me was a curse,
For the gas was took out and electric put in
And the bills I'd pay then was really a sin.

And with TV and such things I was near driv mad,
For m'children just wanted what all their friends had,
And I knew that t'please them I would always be poor,
For the tick-men were never away from m'door.

Well, the years rolled by and with m'children all grown,
And all of them married, w'homes of their own,
I thought I'd have peace, there being just him and me,
But oh dear no, this was not to be.

For a lot of months back, this letter did come,
Which said that my wee house was only a slum,
My lovely wee house, that knowed sad times and bitter,
Was now called a slum, by some City Hall skitter.

Well! I nearly dropped dead where I stood on the floor,
When in comes wee Cassie, m'neighbour next door,
The colour of death and I wasn't much better,
And she had in her hand the very same letter.

The rest of m'neighbours had got letters too,
And seemed that there was nothing at all we could do.
We had protest meetings all over the place,
And we argued until we were blue in the face.

But them City Hall ones are a very tough foe,
And the end of it all was, we just had to go,
And the day I was leaving I lingered a while,
Just to be with friends I'd knowed from a chil'.

When I redd out m'wee house, m'heart was real sore,
And I thought that m'house sensed I'd be back there no more,
For the door gave a screech and the windies all shook
As I stood on the footpath t'have m'last look.

Well, they put him an' me in a high rise flat,
With people on this side and people on that,
With people above us and people below,
But not one friendly face in that place did I know.

In my own wee house I could always look out,
And see the wee childer all playing about,
And take m'wee stool and sit at the door,
But in this flat I could see just the sky and the floor.

Then one day last week I went out for a dander,
And they say where the heart lies the feet always wander.
I walked to the street where I'd lived all my life,
First as a child and then as a wife.

When I saw my wee house, I just stood there and cried.
I felt cold all over, and empty inside.
My wee house that had sheltered my family and me,
Was stripped bare and naked for all eyes to see.

The hall door was lying down flat on the floor,
And the kitchen was covered with plaster and stoor.
The slates were all gone, and the rafters as well
And my lovely wee house was now just a shell

Then down the street came this great big crane,
With a big iron ball on a long heavy chain.
It just stopped fernenst me and then swung round,
And my poor helpless house was brought to the ground.

I opened my mouth, but I just couldn't spake,
And I had the same feeling y'get at a wake.
A lifetime of caring had just come to an end,
And I'd just seen the death of a very dear friend.

For my house was a home, a home full of life,
A haven of love in a world full of strife,
A place of comfort, a refuge from pain,
And now it was gone, with one swing of a crane.

I turned on m'heel, and m'legs were shaking.
I walked slowly away with a heart that was breaking,
I went towards that flat with a feeling of dread
And I wished, like my wee house, I wished I was dead.

Seamus Lavery

Since the reversal of the policy to develop high rise apartments, the community spirit is regenerating in inner city Belfast and it is possible to see children playing in the streets and to see something of the old camaraderie that once existed.

Housing redevelopment Sandy Row, Belfast

MISCELLANEOUS SNATCHES OVERHEARD IN MANY PLACES

Quite honestly I do not know what to make of some of this, but I enjoyed it!

'Ah wus sittin' in the middle of me dinner when ar Sadie put 'er head thru the dur. Seys she til me, "For God's sake hurry up with yon sausage an' come an' have a luk at ar Alfie and ar Willie in the scullery."

Ah finished me dinner an' nipped in next dur til see wot the matter wos.

An there they wos, sittin' in the scullery drinkin'! "Smile," seys Ah, "Yur on Candid Camera!" Ah thought they wos celebrating, but be jabbers, they wus drownin' thur sarrars. Thur team had lost the match. Talk about depression. Willie tuk wan luk at me an' disappeared up them thar stars an' started tho'ing rings 'roun' him. Men! Thur just beg childer! Thur alwus lukin' for symphony!'

'Do yew see thon Mellony? She tuk bad on Sat-ter-day night. She wos turrible bad with her stomach. She was rushed into 'ospitable and ended up in entensive cur. She had tubes everywhere! AND the baby had to be born by sectarian section.'

'Do yew see thon woman thonder? Shiz like me. She wus born on the lower Ormeau. Bat she's forgot her common oridgeens. She married money and has gone to live on the Malone Road. Shiz as common as

Pubs are good places for crack, Morrison's, Bedford Street

durt. She wus my best frien' at school bat she won't talk to me nye. Shiz nathin' bat a jumped up nathin'! Shiz got a conseveratary on the side of 'er house and shiz putting a swimming pool intil it, bat my husband sez it's nathin' bat a sheep dip"

'Do yew see me? See my modesty? Ah've lost it since Ah started attending thon 'ospitable.'

'Ar Sammy had til start attending the 'ospitable. He wus tauld til bring a sample. He put the sample in an auld whiskey bottle and put it in til his pocket. He went til the 'ospitable in the bus and when he put his han in til his pocket til giv it til the nurse it had gone. He'd been pickpocketed!'

Passer-by to man who was tinkering with the engine of his car by the kerbside of a busy road. 'Has yur car stopped starting?'
    'No! It's started stopping!'

'Ar wee Shuey had a urinary infection and he had til go til the dactars. An' seys the dactar, seys he, "When yew go does it light up at the tip?" Ar wee Shuey jest luked the dactar in the eye and as bold as brass seys he til the dactar, seys he, "Dactar, Ah don't know! Ah've niver held a match til it"'

'He wus that ill he wus putt on infedility allowance.'

'My emergency 'eater's nat workin' an' the electric man sez he can't fix it til next week. I don't feel too hot about havin' til wash in cauld water.'

'Ar Jemmy's got a great job. He's on the corporation brush.'

Sometimes the language of young

On the corporation brush

18

people in Belfast and indeed in the rest of Ireland, sounds monotonous because every other word appears to be that naughty one that rhymes with duck and muck but which has gained respectability since the days of my youth and is now in the latest version of the Oxford English Dictionary. Listen carefully for underneath the disguise the rich descriptive flow is still there!

One young person to another on Citybus.

'Are yew goin' til the *ing christenin'?'
'Naw.'
'Why ar yew nat *ing goin'? Do yew nat *ing fancy 'er no more?'
'Naw.'
'Why? Wots *ing wrong wif 'er?'
'Away * yersel! She's got a *ing face like a *ing chewed toffee!'
'Shasn't!'
'Shas an all!'
'She *ing hasn't!'
'She *ing has!'
'Yew *ing have til go til the christenin'.'
'Ah *ing haven't!'
'Why won't yew go til the *ing christenin'?'
'Ah *ing haven't been *ing asked .'
'Yew haven't been *ing asked til the *ing christenin'? Yew ain't *ing goin' til the *ing christenin'! * yew an' yur the *ing faher!'

Two teenage girls to one another on another Citybus.

'Do yew fancy him?'
'* arf!'
'* yersel' Ah think yew *ing fancy him!'
'Yew *ing think Ah *ing fancy 'im? * yew! Ar yew *ing arf yur *ing skull? *ing fancy *ing 'im?!!!! He's that *ing spotty 'is *ing face is like the *ing inside of a *ing peanut bar!'

TROUBLED TIMES

Belfast has had its share of 'troubles' including the recent civil unrest, the I.R.A. campaign of the fifties, the Blitz of the Second World War, the 'Troubles' of the twenties and so on. No matter how great the trouble, the spirit of the people is such that they will always see a funny side.

ANYBODY WANT TO BUY A BOTTLE OF WINDY CLEANER?

Cecil Brennan was a clergy-man who worked Belfast during the blitz. He told of overhearing a conversation between a big fat woman who worked as a cleaner in the Royal Victoria Hospital and one of the porters.

The minute the woman appeared, the porter, who knew there had been several bomb explosions in the street where she lived during the previous night's blitz, shouted over to her,

"Bout ye?"

'Dead on!' replied the woman. 'Only one problem! Know anyone who wants to buy a big bottle of windy cleaner cheap?'

STOP AGGRAVATING THEM !

Cecil also told of an hospitable motherly woman who lived in north Belfast. When the siren sounded warning of the approach of bombers many people used to crowd into her house and shelter either under the stairs or under her heavy wooden table.

One night the children became restless during a particularly awful air raid. The mother crawled out from under the table and began to make a 'wee drap av tea'. Her youngest son stopped being frightened and began running backwards and forwards to the front door with his shirt tails flying, thumbing his nose at the aeroplanes in the sky above and shouting abuse. Eventually the mother caught him, hit him a clout across the ear and shouted, 'Will you come in to hell outta that! Do ye not think they're bad enough without you aggravating them?'

THEY AIN'T EXACTLY THROWIN' MEAT PIES

Apparently there was a wee woman who lived up the Shankill. Once when the sirens sounded to warn of the beginning of an air raid, she and her husband leapt out of bed, threw on their clothes and shot out of the front door of their wee house as if shot from a bullet. Half way up the street the woman stopped and exclaimed, 'I've forgotten my false teeth!' She turned to go back and get them. Her husband grabbed her by the hand and pulled her in the direction of the hills, 'For God's sake come on! Them bombers ain't exactly throwin' meat pies!'

Them bombers ain't exactly throwin' meat pies!'

When Raymond Calvert wrote the 'Ballad of William Bloat' he displayed the humour, defiance and pride shown by Belfast people during times of adversity when it requires a special brand of courage to laugh.

THE BALLAD OF WILLIAM BLOAT

In a mean abode on the Shankill Road
Lived a man called William Bloat.
He had a wife, the bane of his life,
Who continually got his goat.
So one day at dawn, with her nightdress on,
He cut her bloody throat.

With a razor gash he settled her hash,
Oh never was a crime so quick,
But the steady drip on the pillow slip
Of her lifeblood made him sick,
And the pool of gore on the bedroom floor
Grew clotted, cold and thick.

And yet he was glad he'd done what he had,
When she lay there stiff and still,
But a sudden awe of an angry law
Struck his soul with an icy chill,
So to finish the fun so well begun,
He resolved himself to kill.

Then he took the sheet off his wife's cold feet,
And made it into a rope,
And he hanged himself from the pantry shelf,
It was an easy end we hope.
In the face of death with his last cold breath
He solemnly cursed the Pope.

But the strangest turn to the whole concern
Is only just beginning.
He went to hell, but his wife got well,
And is still alive and sinning,
For the razor blade was German made,
But the sheet was Irish linen.

Raymond Calvert

(Recent adaptations of 'The Ballad of William Bloat' by others sometimes refer to the 'razor blade' as 'foreign' rather than German made.)

In more recent times, at the beginning of civil unrest in the late 1960's, Orange processions were banned in Norn Iron on the grounds that they caused division within the population. Crawford Howard imagined Orangemen transporting their customs to foreign places and inspiring people of other lands. He sat down and wrote 'The Arab Orange Lodge'

THE ARAB ORANGE LODGE
(This poem may be sung to the air: 'The Wearing of the Green')

A loyal band of Orangemen from Ulster's lovely land,
They could not march upon the 12th—processions was all banned,
So they flew off till the Middle East this dreadful law to dodge
And they founded in Jerusalem the Arab Orange Lodge

Big Ali Bey who charmed the snakes
   he was the first recruit,
John James McKeag from Portglenone
   learned him till play the flute
And as the oul' Pied Piper was once
   followed by the rats
There followed Ali till the lodge ten
   snakes in bowler hats.

*The speeches at the 'field' that
day were really something new*

They made a martial picture as they marched along the shore.
It stirred the blood when Ali played 'The fez my father wore'
And Yussef Ben Mohammed hit the 'lambeg' such a bash
It scared the living daylights from a camel in a sash!

Now the movement spread both far and wide—there were lodges by the score.
The 'Jerusalem Purple Heroes' was the first of many more
The 'Loyal Sons of Djeddah' and the Mecca Purple Star'
And the 'Rising Sons of Jericho' who came by motor car.

The banners too were wonderful and some would make you smile
—King Billy on his camel as he splashed across the Nile—
But the Tyre and Sidon Temperance had the best one of them all
For they had a lovely picture of Damascus Orange Hall!

The Apprentice boys of Amman marched beneath the blazing sun,
The Royal Black Preceptory were Negroes every one
And Lodges came from Egypt, from the Abu Simbel Falls,
And they shouted 'No surrender!' and 'We'll guard old Cairo's walls!'

But when the ban was lifted and the lodges marched at last
The Arabs all decided for till march right through Belfast
And they caused a lot of trouble before they got afloat,
For they could not get the camels on the bloody Heysham boat!

Now camels choked up Liverpool and camels blocked Stranaer
And the Sheik of Kuwait came along in his great big motor car,
But the 'Eastern Magic' L.O.L. they worked a crafty move.
They got on their magic carpets and flew into Aldergrove!

When they came to Castle Junction where once stood the wee Kiosk,
They dug up Royal Avenue to build a flamin' mosque
And Devlin says to Gerry Fitt, 'I think we'd better go!
There's half a million camels coming down from Sandy Row.'

The speeches at the 'field' that day were really something new,
For some were made in Arabic and some were in Hebrew,
But just as Colonel Nasser had got up to sing 'The Queen',
I woke up in my bed at home and found it was a dream!

Crawford Howard

There followed Ali till the lodge ten snakes in bowler hats

HALF TIME!

Etta Kerr was one of the residents of Ainsworth Avenue which runs from the Protestant Shankill Road through to a Catholic area. In other words, it was a flash point and eventually the ill named 'Peace Line' cut Ainsworth Avenue in two. In the late 60's there were riots outside Etta's for weeks until security measures began to take effect.

Most of the houses in Ainsworth Avenue were of the terrace type, opening directly unto the street and the residents of the Avenue had a difficult time because during riots the front windows of their houses were in danger of being broken and the security forces used C.S. gas to disperse the rioters. The gas not only had an unpleasant effect on rioters, but seeped into houses through broken windows and down chimneys. As Etta said, 'I wish them ones wud go and riot outside thur own front durs and lave usons in peace." During that difficult period house occupiers slept in back bedrooms because, as Etta said, they 'were less likely to be hit a clout on the head by a stone flying through the windy in the middle of the night!'

One night Etta was attempting to ignore the noise coming from the riot at the front of her house and sleep in her back bedroom. The noise was deafening. It rose and fell as the rioters moved up and down the street and as the battle increased and decreased in intensity. Eventually the security forces must have decided their best option was to fire a round of C.S. gas. The gas can have a serious effect of people with asthma and other respiratory problems so the security forces always blew a whistle before using the gas to give people who were sensitive to it the chance to get out of the way. About three o'clock in the morning the whistle blew. Etta was in fear and trembling but she could not keep from laughing in the darkness of her room. She heard some wag among the rioters shout 'Half time lads!'

I wish them ones wud go and riot outside thur own front durs and lave usons in peace

TERRIBLE TALES

I am indebted to Robert McDevitte, David Erwin, Jean Napier, Ronnie Ballard, Owen Kelly and other friends, who swear blind they will sue me if I acknowledge them, for the following terrible tales.

McGUFFY'S PRIZE WINNING PIG

'My friend McGuffy, I don't know where he came from, had a pig that won many prizes in agricultural shows.

Well, one day, McGuffy was brushing the pig down and generally prettying it up for show when he put his had in his pocket to pull out his handkerchief and three fivers, which he had forgotten he'd shoved in his pocket, fell out on to the ground. The pig was greedier and quicker than a banker with an umbrella in June, it lit upon the fivers and gobbled them up.

McGuffy was very upset. After all, money doesn't exactly grow on trees, and I'm talking about the days when a fiver was a fiver, a reckonable amount of money. McGuffy took the pig to the vet who suggested an immediate operation.

McGuffy was appalled. "But you can't do that" he protested, "Isn't he a PRIZE pig. Surely you must be able to do something else?"

McGuffy's plea hung in the air like the stench of bacon behind the Synagogue. Then the vet suddenly remembered, "Well, there is!" says he, "There's an old wives' tale that if you give a pig a large whiskey followed by a smart kick in the rear the pig will cough up, so to speak. It's worth a try!"

So my friend McGuffy walked into Lavery's pub with the pig trotting behind him on a rope. Now Mr. Lavery prided himself on running a clean pub and was about to object when McGuffy shouted, "Large whiskey please!"

Well, business is business! McGuffy turned to the pig, grabbed its snout and with the faintest hint of a deadly threat, said, "Open yer gub!"

As soon as the whiskey had gone down, McGuffy kicked the pig, but good. The pig gave a lurch and began to hiccup, and from the corner of his mouth emerged, yes, a five pound note!!!

"Well' Bless my soul!" said a little weeshy downy bit of a man sat there in the corner of the bar. "Bless us all! That's a wonderful animal you've got there. I'll tell you straight. I'll give you £100 for that pig!"

McGuffy, affronted, informed the wee man in the corner that this was a prize pig and not for sale.

"Large whiskey!" shouts McGuffy twice more not forgetting to kick the pig and on each occasion the animal coughed up a fiver.

The little man in the corner got more and more excited and eventually shouted out, "A thousand pounds for that pig and that's my last word!"

"Done!" exclaims McGuffy, spitting on his hands and pocketing the money.

That is the true story of the remarkable way in which my friend McGuffy managed to sell one pig for a thousand pounds.

Incidentally, do you know what the little man got? Six months hard labour for kicking a drunk pig to death!'

THE CONSTIPATED MAN

Just after the Second World War a wee man who lived on the Newtownards Road near the Holywood Arches became very, very constipated. He went to the doctor, who prescribed a remedy, but it did not do any good.

Eventually, in desperation, he confided his problem to a friend.

The friend was both helpful and sympathetic. 'I have heard,' he said, 'there is a great wee woman who lives in Belmore Street in Enniskillen and that she has a cure for constipation.'

'What good is that to me?' groaned the man. 'I live in Belfast and it's desperate far to Enniskillin.'

'You could go in the bus,' replied the friend as few people in Belfast had cars at that period of time.

'I cud an' all,' replied the man,' and it wud take me all day. I don't fancy goin' all that way on a bus.'

A week passed without relief and the man became more and

more uncomfortable. Eventually he decided there was nothing for it but to travel into the city centre and catch a bus to Enniskillen.

On arriving in Enniskillen he made inquiries and found the woman with the cure for constipation. He knocked on her door. 'Come on, on in,' she shouted. 'Wud ye like a wee cup of tea in yer han?'

'No thank yew,' replied the man, 'It's far too much trouble.'

'Ah, cum on,' coaxed the woman, 'It's naybor at all.'

'Oh! No, thank you. It's really too much trouble.'

'Oh - git on with you. It's naybor. Shur Ah wus about to have a wee cup mesel in me han!'

'Oh! In that case if yur shure it's naybor,' replied the man, 'I'd luv a wee cup of tea in me han.'

The pair sat cracking about the weather in front of fire for about half an hour when suddenly the woman looked the man in the eye and said, 'Ah can see yew've got bother. Yew can't go, can yew?'

'No,' replied the man. 'Ah've no been for about ten days.'

'Well,' replied the woman in a comforting fashion, ' Yew've cum til the right place. Ah can help yew.'

She went into the scullery and came back carrying a tray with a bowl of foul smelling liquid, a bottle and a ladle on it. She put the tray on the table in front of the window and used the ladle to half fill the bottle with the liquid. She turned towards the man. 'Did yew cum by cyar or bus?' she asked.

'Ah came on the bus,' came the reply.

'Yew said yew live on the Newtownards Road,' stated the woman. 'Do yew live near Dee Street?'

'Ah live near the Holywood Arches,' replied the man.

The woman appeared thoughtful. She picked the bottle up, studied it for a few minutes, then poured about a teaspoon of liquid out. She held it up to the light, then added three drops. 'Where is yur toilet?' she asked. 'Is it upstairs or downstairs?'

'Actually it's out the back yard,' came the response. The woman added another drop of liquid to the bottle.

'Now! Last question! Are yew a buttons man or a zip man?'

'Ah'm a buttons man,' replied the man blushing slightly.

Do you know - that was a great wee woman! She was only one button wrong!

INTERESTING PLACES

A man went into Gardner's book shop in Botanic Avenue. He looked at the wide range of magazines on display and eventually turned to a shop assistant for help. 'Have you got a copy of *"The National Geographic Magazine"*?' he asked.

'No,' replied the girl, 'I am afraid it is out of stock.'

'Well,' asked the man, 'Do you have a copy of *"Playboy"*?'

'I am really sorry,' replied the girl, 'I am afraid it is also out of stock.'

The man turned towards the door and the girl felt curious, 'Excuse me?' she queried. 'I am interested in your choice of magazine. Surely there is a tremendous contrast between *"The National Geographic Magazine"* and *"Playboy"*?'

'Not at all,' replied the man. 'I just like looking at photographs of places I am never going to be able to explore.'

Queen's Elms near Botanic Avenue

HELLUCINATIONS

During the First World War a soldier from Norn Iron became separated from his patrol in the Sahara Desert. He was very much in love with a good looking girl from Belfast to whom he had recently become engaged so he was determined to survive.

He walked and walked and walked for three days and three nights in the direction of the Army camp. Eventually he became so weak and exhausted he could walk no more so he crawled on his hands and knees for three days and three nights. He became even more weak and exhausted and could not crawl. He lay still for a few minutes after which the stubborn genes in his Norn Iron ancestry exerted themselves and he began to inch towards the camp on his stomach. He lifted his head and looked up. Suddenly he could see the sea. And what was that coming out of the sea? It was a beautiful curvaceous woman, wearing a low cut silken gown which stuck to every luscious line of her body. She smiled at him. 'Soldier', she asked, 'do yew fancy a feg?'

'Mrs!' he replied, 'Do Ah wot? Ah haven't had a feg for about three weeks. Ah've got withdrawal symptoms!'

The woman smiled, reached into her cleavage, produced a packet of Gallagher's blues and a box of matches. She placed the feg between her ruby lips, lit it, had a puff, then transferred it to the soldier's mouth.

The soldier was in ecstasy. He pulled on the cigarette. 'Thanks Mrs,' he sighed. 'That's the best fag Ah've ever had.'

*Entry off Ann Street,
Inner City Belfast*

The woman smiled, 'Well soldier' she grined, 'how about a drink?'

'Are yew kiddin'?' asked the soldier, 'Ah'd almost give my right arm for a drink.'

The woman put her hand down her cleavage and produced a delicate cut glass and a bottle of the best Bushmills single malt whiskey. She poured a stiff drink into the glass and held it to the soldier's mouth. He was in ecstasy! 'Mrs!' he murmured, 'that's the best drink Ah've had in the whole of my life!'

The woman smiled in a contented fashion. 'Soldier' she asked, 'would yew like to play around?'

'Mrs dear!' he gasped, 'Don't tell me yew've got a bag and a set of clubs down there as well?'

BELLEVUE ZOO'S INTELLECTUAL MONKEY

A monkey at Bellevue Zoo became very intellectual. It learnt to read and to have deep philosophical discussions with its keeper. It became fascinated with religion and read the Bible from cover to cover.

One day the keeper brought the monkey a copy of *'Darwin's Theory of Evolution'* and gave it to him, saying as he did so, 'You should read that. I think you'll find it interesting.' The monkey was fascinated. He read *Darwin's Theory of Evolution* from cover to cover. The next day the keeper found the monkey standing in the middle of his cage with a thoughtful look on his face and the *Bible* in one hand and *'Darwin's Theory of Evolution'* in the other. 'Why,' asked the keeper, ' are you standing in the centre of your cage holding the *Bible* in one hand and *'Darwin's Theory of Evolution'* in the other?'

'Because' replied the monkey, 'I'm just trying to work out if I'm my brother's keeper or my keeper's brother.'

A DIRTY OLD MAN?

I could ignore it, if only it would stop eating my potato crisps

One Friday an old farmer came in from the country and bought a gosling, which he tucked under his arm and then dandered around the town. Eventually it began to rain and he decided to go to a matinee performance at a cinema. He realised that animals are not allowed into cinemas so he visited the toilet opposite the City Hall and tucked the gosling neatly down his trousers.

On entering the cinema he settled himself down comfortably in the back row and proceeded to enjoy the show. The gosling felt cramped down the man's trousers, worked at the zip until it opened, stuck its head out and watched the big screen. The bird appeared quiet and content so the farmer did not interfere with it. A young couple came into the cinema, sat down beside the farmer and began eating potato crisps. After a few minutes the girl became very agitated. She hit her boyfriend a dig in the ribs and pointed at the farmer. 'Look at that,' she whispered.

'Oh! Don't pay any attention to that,' responded the boyfriend. 'Dirty old men often come into cinemas. They are harmless. Just don't take him or it under your notice.'

'I could ignore it,' replied the girl, 'if only it would stop eating my potato crisps.'

WHAT A COST!

Wee Willie worked down at the shipyard. He was a joiner who had a big burly mate called Arti and a big ferocious wife called Aggie who abused him in a terrible fashion.

One day Wee Willie came into work and he was limping.

'What happened to you?' asked a concerned Arti.

33

'Aggie was annoyed with me last night,' came the reply. 'I was out cutting the lawn and the phone rang. I rushed into the house and I forgot to wipe my feet. I got some grass cuttings on the carpet. Aggie was FURIOUS and kicked my shins.'

'That's a terrible woman of yours,' stated Arti. 'You'd be much better off without her.'

'I would an' all,' replied Wee Willie glumly, 'but there's nothing much I can do about her.'

Next day Willie came into work and he had his arm in a sling.

'She didn't, did she?' queried Arti.

'She did indeed,' replied Willie.

'Why?' asked Arti.

'It was this way - I was cleaning the windows last night and I didn't notice a couple of streaks. Aggie was FURIOUS. She grabbed me by the arm and threw me on the ground and jumped on me. She dislocated my shoulder and I'm all covered in bruises. I'm all sore, I'm telling ye. If she hadn't been at home I'd have taken a day off work.'

'That woman is a pest,' snarled Arti. 'You should hire a killer. You'd be better off without her.'

'You're right!' said Willie, 'I'd be much better off without her, but I can't afford to hire a killer and she is much bigger than me. If I tried to do it myself, she'd kill me! It would be dangerous!'

'I see what you mean,' said Arti.

Next day Willie came in to work and he had two lovely black eyes.

Arti was enraged. 'Did SHE do that to you?' he exploded.

'Who's SHE? The Cat?' replied Willie, making a faint attempt at a joke.

'IT'S NO JOKING MATTER,' roared Arti. 'TELL ME WHAT HAPPENED.'

Willie explained, 'Last night I was washing the dishes and one of the good china cups fell out of my hand and smashed on the floor. She was FURIOUS! She lifted the fists and blacked my eyes.'

'That woman is awful!' exclaimed Arti. 'She does not deserve to live. I told you you should hire a killer.'

'Where would I get the money to hire a killer?' asked Willie. 'I'm only allowed £1 a week pocket money.'

'That woman should not be allowed to live,' stressed Arti. 'Tell you what - I'll kill her. She is a waste of space, in fact worse than that. She is worse than a waste of space because she is using up oxygen. It would be a pleasure to kill her. I'll do it for nothing.'

'I couldn't let you do it for nothing,' protested Willie. 'It would be on my conscience. Tell you what. I'll give you all the money I have £1.'

'Right you are,' replied Arti, pocketing the £1. 'Where do I find thon woman?'

'She's working in "Crazy Prices" on a check-out desk this morning,' came the reply.

'Right!' said Arti, 'The sooner the job's done, the sooner it will be over.' He strode out of the shipyard, down the road and into "Crazy Prices". He saw Aggie on a check-out desk, rushed over in a temper and started to choke her. Two of her friends attempted to rescue her. Arti was in such a rage he choked all three of them. Next day a Belfast newspaper bore the headline, '"Crazy Prices" Artichokes three for £1!'

Where do I find thon woman

THE INDUSTRIAL SCENE

It was once said locally that Belfast had the biggest single ship yard in the world (Harland and Wolff), the biggest rope works in the world and one of the finest aeroplane industries in the world! Times have changed but the city is still dominated by shipyard cranes. At the present time the two largest cranes enable the ship yard to repair and construct oil 'super-tankers', the largest ships in the world! The cranes are called 'Goliath' and 'Samson'. Goliath is very slightly smaller than Samson and is a few years older. The habit of giving objects names is one enjoyed by residents of Belfast. For instance, the statues on the Ulster Bank in Shaftesbury Square are known locally as 'Draft' and 'Overdraft' and the American War Memorial

Statues on the Ulster Bank known locally as 'Draft' and 'Overdraft'

American War Memorial known locally as 'the dog's delight'

outside the City Hall, whose clean modern lines contrast strangely with the older statues in the grounds, was once named 'the dog's delight'!

Ships, as well as cranes, once dominated the city. Belfast people were very aware of whatever ship happened to be in the course of construction at the time and took a pride in the finished product and an interest in its fate. The ill-fated Titanic was built in Belfast and launched in 1912. Old people who can remember it being built and launched recount the pride ship workers, and indeed the entire population of Belfast, took in the vessel. When it sank, the city went into mourning. People stood weeping in the streets, women donned mourning clothes, the men wore black ties and black arm-bands, black bows were tied to door knockers and shop windows were dressed with black crepe.

During the war, Belfast people had a caring attitude to fighting ships built 'in the yard'. Of course, at that time every ship lost at sea caused concern as each loss seemed to increase the threat of invasion. However, each 'Belfast' ship either damaged or sunk gave rise to heightened feelings of concern and those returning for repair were warmly welcomed.

There are many stories, jokes and monologues associated with 'the yard'. Crawford Howard's 'Diagonal Steam Trap' is a local favourite.

THE DIAGONAL STEAMTRAP

Now they built a big ship down in Harland's —
She was made for to sell to the Yanks
And they called on the Yard's chief designer
To design all the engines and works.

Now finally the engines was ready
And they screwed in the very last part
An' yer man says, 'Let's see how she runs, lads!'
An' bejasus! the thing wouldn't start!

So they pushed and they worked an' they footered
An' the engineers' faces got red
And the designer he stood lookin' stupid
An' scratchin' the back of his head.

But while they were fiddlin' and workin'
Up danders oul' Jimmie Dalzell.
He had worked twenty years in the 'Island'
And ten in the 'aircraft' as well.

So he pushed and he worked and he muttered,
Till he got himself through till the front
And he has a good look roun' the engine
An' he gives a few mutters and grunts,

And then he looks up at the Gaffer
An' says he, 'Mr. Smith, d'ye know?
They've left out the Diagonal Steam Trap!
How the hell d'ye think it could go?'

Now the engineer eyed the designer
And the designer he looks at the 'hat'
And they whispered the one to the other,
'Diagonal Steam Trap? What's that?'

But the Gaffer, he wouldn't admit like
To not knowin' what this was about,
So he says, 'Right enough, we were stupid!
The Diagonal Steam Trap's left out!'

Now in the meantime oul' Jimmie had scarpered
—away down to throw in his boord—
And the Gaffer comes up and says, 'Jimmy!
D'ye think we could have a wee word.'

'Ye see that Diagonal Steam Trap?
I know it's left out — it's bad luck,
But the engine shop's terrible busy
D'ye think ye could knock us one up?'

Now, oul' Jimmy was laughin' his scone off.
He had made it all up for a geg
He seen what was stoppin' the engine—
The feed-pipe was blocked with a reg!

But he sticks the oul' hands in the pockets
An' he says, 'Aye, I'll give yez a han'.
I'll knock yez one up in the mornin'
An' the whole bloody thing will be grand!'

So oul' Jim starts to work the next morning
To make what he called a Steam Trap,
An oul' box an' a few bits of tubing
An a steam gauge stuck up on the top,

An' he welds it all on till the engine
And he says till the wonderin' mob,
'As long as that gauge is at zero
The Steam Trap is doin' its job!'

Then he pulls the reg outa the feed pipe
An, he gives the oul' engine a try
An' 'bejasus! she goes like the clappers
An' oul Jimmy remarks, 'That's her nye!'

Now the ship was the fastest seen ever,
So they sent her away till the Turks
But they toul' them, 'That Steam Trap's a secret!
We're the only ones knows how that works!

'But the Turk's they could not keep their mouths shut
An' soon the whole story got roun'
An' the Russians got quite interested —
Them boys has their ears till the groun'!

So they sent a spy dressed as a sailor
To take photies of Jimmy's Steam Trap
And they got them all back till the Kremlin
An' they stood round to look at the snaps.

Then the head spy says, 'Mr Kosygin!
I'm damned if I see how that works!'
So they sent him straight off to Siberia
An' they bought the whole ship from the Turks!

When they found the Steam Trap was a 'cod, like'
They couldn't admit they'd been had,
So they built a big factory in Moscow
To start makin' Steam Traps like mad!

Now Kosygin rings up Mr. Nixon
And he says, 'Youse'uns thinks yez are great!
But wi' our big new Russian-made Steam trap
Yez'll find that we've got yez all bate! '

Now oul Nixon, he nearly went 'harpic,
So he thought he'd give Harland's a call
And he dialled the engine-shop number
And of course he got sweet bugger all!

But at last the call came through to Jimmy
In the midst of a terrible hush,
'There's a call for you here from the "White House
Says oul' Jim, 'That's a shop in Portrush!'

There's a factory outside of Seattle
Where they're turnin' out Steam Traps like Hell
It employs twenty-five thousand workers
And the head of it — Jimmy Dalzell!

Crawford Howard

'WE'VE GOT TO BE DEAD ON, SIR!

It is said that when the shipyard was taken over by a German company some years ago, the German executives were anxious to know the degree of skill possessed by the Belfast workforce. They questioned one of the workers, asking, 'Can you work to percentages of 100% accuracy?'

'100% accuracy?' questioned the worker.

'That's right!' replied the potential owner.

'100% accuracy, that's nathin',' replied the worker. 'We've got to be "dead on", Sir!'

We've got to be "dead on", Sir!'

THE MYSTERIOUS WHEELBARROW

According to local legend, once upon a time there was a shipyard worker who was a real conundrum. He appeared to be a conscientious good worker, well liked and respected by his colleagues and on the same rate of pay as all the other workers in his section. However, he had a vastly superior life style, when compared with the rest of those employed by the yard. He appeared, on the surface anyway, to be as wealthy as a gaffer.

The fact that the man had money to burn eventually became evident to the security guards who searched him every day before he left to go home. Each day the man came to the gate pushing an empty wheelbarrow, the guards looked at it very carefully, but there was never anything in it, so they searched the worker assiduously. Nothing! They could find no evidence of stolen goods which could have been sold to supplement his income.

Other workers became curious about the wealth displayed - the comparatively opulent home, the number of foreign holidays, the possibility of inherited wealth and so on. But no! All the man ever said was, 'I get exactly the same wage as you. The only difference is that my wife's a very good manager.'

'Samson' and 'Goliath'

The other workers started to wonder if his wife could be 'on the game.' But the woman was as ugly as sin, went to church three times on a Sunday and had never been blemished by even a breath of scandal, so that seemed unlikely.

After many years, the wealthy worker reached retirement age. On his last day at work, the security guards went through the familiar ritual of searching the man and his wheelbarrow. Eventually they said, 'We know you are smuggling something. We can't prove it and we are really curious. If we give you 10 quid between us and promise not to take any action, will you tell us what you were smuggling out of the yard?'

'Are you sure you will take no action?' asked the man.

'Certain' replied the guards. 'We will reward you because it will help prevent others try the same trick.'

'Right!' replied the man, 'I'll tell you. I was smuggling wheelbarrows. The wife sold them through her brother's shop. The brother thought I made wheelbarrows in my spare time and I have a wee workshop at home to give that impression. All I ever did was remove all signs of identity and I had a nice little earner. The brother done good as well as he sold the barrows cheap!'

THE TWENTY FOUR SEATER CRANE

There once was a crane in the yard which caused puzzlement among the managers. It was extremely popular with the workers at lunch time. Every lunch hour saw a scramble with men competing to climb up on the crane and sit gazing over the boundary into Shorts Aircraft factory with their boxes of sandwiches and billycans of tea.

Eventually, one of the gaffers decided to find out what was going on. He pushed through the crowds, using his 'hat' to queue-skip, climbed up on the crane and looked over the boundary into Shorts. He was puzzled. He had a good view into one of the manager's offices but it was uninteresting. Then the door of the office opened and in came a pretty young secretary. Both she and the manager took their clothes off and began doing unmentionable things to each other on top of the desk and the mystery was solved!

Crawford Howard was inspired one night when he was sitting, enjoying a pint, in a pub in east Belfast. A fitter, who was employed by Shorts, came in and began to do some serious drinking, someone in the crowd looked at the fitter and said, 'Yer flyin' tonight!' Crawford sat down and wrote 'The Flying Fitter'.

THE FLYING FITTER

A big lad came to work in the 'Aircraft',
So the lads took him out for some beers,
And soon they were calling him 'Dumbo',
Because of the size of his ears.

But after a couple of hours, like,
They had to face up till the truth.
There wasn't no two ways about it,
Big Dumbo was only a 'drouth'.

He was knockin' back 'half uns' like water,
And wee Jimmy looks up and says 'Hi!
If you take any more ye'll be flyin'!
He sez, 'Listen, oul' han', I CAN fly!

Sez wee Jim, 'D'ye mean yez a pilot?
Well, I just hope that I'll be around,
The next time you're goin' up solo,
When ye get thon big lathe off the ground!'

The big lad says, 'I need no airplane!
Ye see when I go on the tear
An' I get a few bottles an' half 'uns,
I can just go straight up in the air!'

Well the whole place went into hysterics
To think of the very idea
An' the big lad got red in the face, like,
An' he says to wee Jim, 'Houl' my beer!'

Then he takes a buck lep on the counter.
The lads could do nothin' but laugh,
But he gives a few flaps with his ears, like,
And bejasus! the bugger takes aff!

An' before~ ye could knock back a half 'un,
He was buzzin' about roun' the light,
Like a flamin' great moth roun' a lantern
Ye would see on a good summer night

An' then he swoops down on wee Jimmy
An' he snatches the beer front his hand,
An he hovers about roun' the counter
Sez wee Jim, 'He's goin' in for to land!'

But landing was not in his programme
The window was open, you see,
So he flutters straight out through the window
An' shouts 'I'm for Donaghadee!'

Now the lads was all struck wi' amazement.
They said, 'Where has he got till at all?'
Then wee Jim yells, 'Bejasus, I see him!
He has lit on the oul' City Hall!'

And right enough there he was perchin'
About eighty five feet off the ground,
Sharing his 'piece' with the pigeons
And the starlings all flutterin' round.

Says wee Jim, 'We'll sneak up on him aisy!
If you come up too quick he'll take fright.
Put a bottle of beer on the windy
An' mebbe he'll roost there all night!'

But before any of the lads could get near him
He shot away up in the air.
Sez wee Jim, 'I would not have believed it
If I had not of had of been there!'

But yer man he went higher an' higher
Till he disappeared over the town.
Sez wee Jim, 'I still think he's for landin'
For the flaps of his trousers is down!

'Now you've heard of them astronaut Yankees,
They left a wireless set on the moon.
It sends back all oul' daft information
Like if it's going to blow up, an' how soon.

They were sitting one night at Cape Kennedy,
When a fella wi' phones on his head sez,
'There's a voice comin' down from the moon here
But I couldn't make out what it said.'

Then up steps a fella from Belfast
Sez he, 'Sure there's nothin' to that.
It said, "Two by the neck and a half 'un!
And make sure that the half 'un is hot!"

Then the voice in the headphones continued
And said, 'God, but my head's awful thick!
Tell Shorts I'll be in on the Monday,
But till then I will be on the sick!'

Now, it seems that yer man got off coorse like
—That full that he could'nt half see—
An' he found he had lit on the moon, like,
Instead of in Donaghadee!

Now I know of some of you won't believe this.
Ye'll think the whole story's a 'cod'.
It's as true as that Paisley's a 'Mickey'
Or as true as the Pope is a 'Prod'.

Crawford Howard

He's goin' in for to land

THE ONLY PLACE FOR ME

Progress has come to the city and many things have changed since Bill Nesbitt wrote 'The Only Place For Me' in the 1960's. However, the heart and spirit of Belfast people have remained constant so I can do nothing but agree with the sentiments expressed by Bill's monologue.

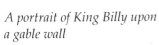

The City Hall

A portrait of King Billy upon a gable wall

Modern replacement of 'wee kiosk' in Castle Junction

THE ONLY PLACE FOR ME

I'll speak to you of Belfast, stranger, if you want to know,
So listen, and I'll tell you why I love this city so…

Belfast is an Ulsterman, with features dour and grim,
It's a pint of creamy porter, a Sunday morning hymn,
A steaming pasty supper, or vinegar with peas,
A little grimy cafe where they serve you 'farm house' teas,
A banner on July the Twelfth, a sticky toffee apple,
An ancient little Gospel Hall, a Roman Catholic chapel,
A 'Telly' boy with dirty face, a slice of apple tart,
A fry upon a Saturday, hot 'coal breek' on a cart,
A Corporation gas-man, complete with bowler hat,
A wee shop on a corner with a friendly bit of chat,
An oul' lad in a duncher, a woman in a shawl,
A pinch of snuff, a tatie farl, a loyal Orange Hall,
A tobacco smell in York Street, a bag of 'yella man',
An Easter egg that's dyed in whin, a slice of Ormo pan,
A youngster with some sprickly-begs inside a wee jam-jar,
A meeting at the Custom House, an old Victorian bar,
Mud banks on the Lagan when the tide is running low,
A man collecting 'refuse', bonfires in Sandy Row,
A bag of salty dullis, a bowl of Irish stew
And goldfish down in Gresham Street, a preacher in a queue,
A portrait of King Billy upon a gable wall,
A flower-seller on a stool outside the City Hall,
A half-moon round a door-step, a 'polisman' on guard,
A pedlar crying 'Delph for Regs!', a little white washed yard…

And there's your answer, stranger, and now I'm sure you'll see
Why Belfast is the only place in all the world for me.

Bill Nesbitt